11/17

THE PRACTICE OF RESIDUE

KIMBERLY LYONS

THE PRACTICE OF RESIDUE

SUBPRESS · 2012

AUTHOR'S NOTE

A set of the stanzas of "Practice of Residue" were
first published as: *Restorative Analects* (Envelope 8, 2004).
With gratitude to David Abel.

A subsequent set of these stanzas were published as
Selections from Restorative Analects (Unarmed chapbook, 2006).
Thank you, Michael Mann.

The author would like to thank Jackson Highfill for patience and
interest, Daniel Bouchard and the Subpress Collective, Julian
Talamanetz Brolaski for editorial assistance, Toni Simon for the
artistic consultation and acts of kindness, Michael Russem of Kat
Ran Press, Elizabeth Robinson for sustaining encouragement,
and Vyt Bakaitis, for so much more.

"The Last Flower on Earth" appeared in
The Poetry Project Newsletter (Dec/Jan 2012).
Many thanks to Paul Foster Johnson.
Language from *Divigations* by Stéphane Mallarmé
(trans. by Barbara Johnson) and
The Secret Book of Boys by Conn and Hall Iggulden
are quoted in the poem "Secret Ink."

ISBN: 978-1-930068-53-7

Library of Congress Control Number: 2012938274

Cover art: Toni Simon

Subpress Books are distributed by Small Press Distribution.
www.spdbooks.org

\

For Lynn Behrendt and Anne Gorrick, and Toni Simon

CONTENTS

Each wolf
one serpent twined
indefinite mother of pearl
I'm cast down, a shipwreck
in the elemental month.
In warm light, I place a box
to endure reduction, shame, the alphabet.

In bed I dwell
straying from the white poplar tree.
Abinito, intoxicating path
weaning from the mother's breast
I abide
one who abets
a lady's maid.

Ceremonial, remote from the mouth
a vowel, a dwelling
of the body
washed off
on fire, name for
loss of will

abreuvoir let the liquid run
forgiveness in the body
suddenly
up to the brim
abrasion (abracadabra) I
made from it absinthe
entire pretext secret

the hedge sparrow
acacia, quality of being
approached
like a hawk sloping upward
space, a new climate.
I deal in accidence
a partner in crime

O accordion, your accelerating
reckoning

in clusters removes weariness
hearing sound
a person whom we know
happens at nightfall

strengthening the action of a medicine
really, part of a play
the rope dancer
forms words
designs on
spheres.

Acquiescence is a
measure of attention in
courtship
small poisonous snake
possessing the first man
inflame speech on a
letter, a gland,
the diamond

adjoin, closely pressed
written ornament is the
dried brick in the sun
who adorns that chest as a
faintly shadowed scorched
bed, aerial weather
a vessel for measuring air

yield affection
flow
insult openly
to pour on
after one heart
with mouth open in wonder
in the west
after sunset

slanting nimble agent
nothing can be known
of things
Sum total, aglimmer

to shiver, living in folds
augustial
the shallow hem
lateral aim
in a dirigible
I flap
a white heron

although albescent
agar a small isle
alchemic
alarm clock
arouse from sleep
Albert

a recess in summer
divert contingencies
a place of Moorish kings.
Watchfulness. Letters & signs
from mouth to anus

alkahest, the Koran
words with the same letter
legs and arms
Moonshine
solvent
assign to

deposited by a flood
lodged in an almond
a beehive, hollow
of the ear
flower that never buds
what is dictated

so be it, I use both hands
for walking in resin
in concealment
liable to be the sign &
in water and on earth.

A fabulous serpent

restorative analects, the body
lay open formed from
anamnesis, pineapple & stamens.

I fix my hopes
on oil of aniseed, those who lived
long ago, clauses, angelolatry,
intricate velocity.

I dislike England, anything English
Annatto.
Lord of the electron cell
you encircle the column.

Before daylight no one
existing prior to the creation
of this world
before dinner
wireless substance that
neutralizes
to free the pulp
from traces

antifebrile choral masque
in inverse
side of the sun
melts sun
in anticipation

leafless, I tend to bees
beg to be
free from spherical
abbreviation
sense & motion
meaning to another

to apply, put close
omitted
senses
a garment

part of the circumference
the plum
Of the zodiac, Arabia
inclined
by the pillars
one who guided
like an eagle's beak

hollow under the shoulder
an aroma
used in early days
sweet arnica
with one hundred eyes

a pointed material order, a dancer
burning strata

looks like the asp or things
secret
sudden
declaration
positively utter
in an oblique way
the practice of residue.

In one's absence, a victory
one degree below
Madagascar
behind the house fed by
its black
flow of rich brocades
hardened by heat

a strip of cloth
is held for
a writer of ballads
a tropical weed &
extrudation
of narrative

body inflated with sugar
is fastening a woman's hair
blow at a pit
mouth a fig
their language

a rind of skin exposed
grain in a fresh
enclosure for baptism a
kind of poet
bears
yellow flowers and
uncultured expression

loaves warming in sunshine
in wicker vessel born
in plaited
music, a bat
a cradle

salt in crystalline men
storing electricity
in an oriental market
a gulf
a recess of the sea

more forward radiant
monk
light a signal
convey
relation

with the finger
enchant whatever pleases
because beatitude
liquid, blood,
came to be
the sign
the dim garden
charm bewitch the
clouds

glossy tree, procreate
bees in the presence of
honey
ask for something

insect producing wax
give rise to
glossy first milk
of time

overladen by darkness
a fabric of small
jewels and soil
particle of music
began the world, start life

current of a stain
writing
into fire
below sorrow
an instrument

orange and lemon in verse
aromatic hem the medication
scatter loosely sparks
spice
think, thrash
besmirched with spittle
cloved the 2nd letter
of the Greek alphabet.

I, a sloped, raw knave
oblique face
between two fires
drink history.
An ox, mourn
the canopy of ladies.
Biangular
spongy, absorbent.
I moisten, perplex
cast.
Drink frequently,
worship books.

The bird of June
the smooth bark
the stuff
conception written
binds a flexible box
joined the owl to
descent
one's body at birth.

Black out with chalk
unglazed bitter
secrets
reveal
in the open air
cloudy small cakes
small pieces of the past.

Black Maria, your soothing
gust of rhymeless verse
lights
obliterate a
heraldic shield.
Unwritten, the bone
of the shoulder.

Become a mixture
exposed, color a
compound of highest
happiness.

Ink on paper
garments spill
lips in flowers
a stitch of blue
for heating flame
a current on the skin
work
desire.

Lady devoted to
a sailor
bell-shaped
exalt the
boat man

cylinder for thread
for singing
the temperature of
prophecy
a door.
North American singing
a horse given to running away

bind a small

composition a book

issues

deep curve

sound floats

across a river

a fire, a nursemaid

insects, great reader

intoxicated

the voltage

God of the North

a hotel

lace

borax

anything that helps

large water worm
a candle
glass for liquids
seek, collect
study
visible limit the
economy system
leafy nook
interior of a basin
an archer, I compress
barking money
destitute of passion, I
braid
enclosing words
with many branches
to bind a hawk's wing

a harsh cask with an alloy of brass
with zinc, a pig's head.
I cry like an ass
secreting vowels
a breviary
who fastened penetrated

square burnt clay
at the end
make tea and boil
a wild rose bush
attend the bridegroom

glittery salt on
the eyelids of a horse
eggs, apple
made of sulfur, hair
a small fish
of Western England
tears, the sea, universal
book

stitched
     paper
wireless silk stuff
be hot
or dusky red
of water, wintry
a fox's tail
brush by

clearing obstruction
apt to float, I burble
at a writing table

a boot, a tragedy
of 8 gallons
burnishing
a state of being

cream by churning
in accordance with
the milk that remains

Lord Byron
a boy who waits
a number 100
Cabaret, Mecca, kabbalah
I work a side passage.

A cablegram
A criolet
A cachou
fall of the voice
in France
as leaves
make tea

a vessel
a heap of stones
flattery
reduce to chalk
succession of Mohammed
writes a beautiful handwriting
an early kind of photography
its motion
camouflage
W.H. Talbot
caix, carving, camisole

to whiten door steps
aromatic, candent
hold the candle
do knowingly
dance
be any way comparable
to him

persevere by coating
canopy of heaven
eating one's own kind
a saint of dogs
encrusted with sugar
hair like seed cake
the shell of a tortoise
the glass bottle
traveling the course of life.

In Norway
four roads meet
at an expanse of grass
bones of the wrist
in map making
one who carries
a female figure
Soft wool of Kashmir
or albumoid
or bird
or book, a mould
to catalyze
sudden calamity
disorder in the eye
remain entangled
rainfall flows in to the river

heavenly blue sky
underground
tree
to overlay
the celebrant
of living matter.

I crawl, wingless
half horse
full of fault finding
a fabulous monster
the last supper
dropping wild wax
of a light red dark blue
in the brain
engraves indelibly
the nether world.

Endless chain of Venus
a goblet I call to
a little songbird
a husk of corn
I preside with disks
make hot by rubbing

a chapel
a narrow sea
I sing a sailor's song
while hauling.

Bawd, procuress, fold the sea
confound with splendor
cover with drips
a lover

make mute, malignity
overtake a house for bees
encircle, stain
benediction
The green bibliography revolving
a kind of gate
for controlling conception

bird of night, telescope with
two eyes
bind such an animal the early
cinematographic birthday blindly
in black and white

membranous black book
related to bitterish discharge
of the blue color
in veins in animals
from the air
blessings with blood a
relationship
absorbent
priest full of bones
who conveys
a page in a book
with a silver spoon

bind with laced knots
the barking of dogs

longing for distilled waters
Wales & England especially Irish
obstacles, sulfur, offspring

a key, raw
in a children's hospital
a lava flow
expulsion of southern Europe
blade fixed in plough

a day in which a wish
for what is unlawful
which couples desire
the old method of writing
a brood of partridges

fall to superfluity
a cave of rhymes
cradle of the cranium
of fissures and black silk
syllables and croaking

separating cream from chalk
I cry "craven" to a reader
a burning king's evil
embattled parapet
at Cremona
a child's bed, translation
used by goldsmiths
between sleep, watches
the world

in bird's gullet
leaves of a withered old woman
or raven or shoemaker
belonging to the lily
shaped chirping
angel who entraps thus:
press into small folds the surface
the ships
the tuft of hair

with four equal
crucibles, cry as a cock
exult in cross examination
treading on holy ground
as the crow flies
with a view

a hidden name forms into a cube-shaped
child, its call
a cipher a
kind of channel, a crystal
edge of the knife

a furnace, cuneal,
a scraping instrument
to become asp-shaped

full of love coagulate
electricity
eager to learn
magical practices
a state of strangeness

the true skin, a hurricane,
circular inky liquid
that makes
the wood pigeons a
a bag of silk
a cymar
which cuts water
The blue
carbon
that cut the Gordian knot
The one-eyed one
who makes
a dog-headed man.

Linger lover, everyday,
the deliciousness of a
moist Russian
narcissus, strike gently
sending letters by post
diffused, be loosely suspended
of infallible
    metrical foot

mark with holes
a beloved daybook
keep on darting
agitating the light of day
inside forever brilliant
absence
mend a soaked
morning star

pour off ornamental sediment
leave behind
a bone
crack by heat a code
removing colors
the distance of the star
the true north decoction
to translate what is unintelligible
the last names falling off

inscribe the void, clear
flowing down
leaves. Subtract,
deflect the course of purification

utter the spirit of
erasing delirious letters
passage
that can be poisonous

extirpation of the artificial
description of water
accumulated matter
to take away from water
the separate part
a tooth
the nude unraveling term's
meaning

the rails of
a waterless traveler's region
descends in to ancestors
medicine tending to
a state of being
commission of derived
lineage, the
undressed

diffluent, the room's
slow position
ripples in water, a process
the delay

two vowels having two petals
dip into
a short bath
by refraction
the diola
a two-handled vase
the circuit of the throat

in describing a curve
wet, windy
strip of hope
expel refusal to believe
produces self control
leave off
deduct from
the stained disorder

spread hair in integral
cohesion
slight pulverizing
out of a grave
cloak the act

who dispenses medicines
at a distance
dilated by pressure from within
divert mental pain
spirit distillation
is drawn in to drops.

Want of union or the quiet of worry
Unclothe by which another
in a giddy forecast
descent into
divination
double reading
under the garb
make deep inquiry

working
by degrees through
what is drained off
array, convert, adorn
in linen
rough documents
further down the stream

extend the swallowing
intoxicated
heart of medieval hum
small particle of
a fall
sink to the ground
write & send
the mail home

a conduit
of the Indian Ocean
two-fold explosive
composition in motion.

Write at dusk
In the course of dark-colored
electricity
ability to endure
imprisonment in
a girl's head
resisting duties
an underground cell
dulcimer
filled with dust

The sun rises
water dripping
black ebony earring
in the earth, vulcanized
horizon
velocity projecting
resurrection

echo
edge of a whirlpool
intercept
utterable
interposition of another

in the egg an oval body
effulgent
the discharging
thread

omission of words
electrons to complete
lengthening
    clotted
draw out any of the four
elements of the eleventh hour
with her lover of physics
and animal

·

fold in the arms
embrocate red work
entangle
small piece
in dying fire
fasten oblivion

glasslike bright green
spark
suspended in it, play
heaven of pure fire
state of being empty
redden it.

An act on the skin
lettering on the branches
of liquid
give to all glands
enduring
compiler of the encyclopedia.

Art of cutting
border with semi circular indents
puzzling little person. Bind with fetters
absorb moisture, make hard
enfold in spirit, polygon with nine sides.
     Knots entrap
set of nine.
Enough and enough, more
knots. Insert
name in a shrine of green
sword shaped books.
Enthrill difficulties
enshroud the architecture of
the insect.

In its flow, one enters
the door of clouds.
The outskirts
at the root of the tongue.
Inscription on
age of moon on January 1.

Like an almanac
a poem of the science of
tears of the prevalent
transitory ornamental particular.

The falling disease.

Opaque lantern
perplexed the great circle.
Equilibrist
dress for January
Projecting lyric requisites.

Write a hermit corrosive
chronology.
Messenger boy, sooner
than a wheel is
connected, form in to an escarp.
Abstain from escape. Shield
with perfume with
beer, wine and coffee
that boiling agitation
that has existed
will always exist
a kind of vessel
of human development of ancient
smoothness of sounds. Eurterpe,
make empty
the evanescent gospel, vanishing
evening always turning
into vapor.

In layers being breathed outside the tribe
unmask
discourse, cast off skin of
the intrinsic
hair in eyelids, the Latin
fact woven
on the face. Be opposite,
eye beam
on the sun's surface.
Invent a small circuit.

Stammer, disappear gradually
a bundle of shocks, for these
fall away
in rumor, drop of
overpowerings.
Fairy land, the
void
Of a grotesque dreamer. Respectfully,
green is predominant. The background
is yellow, remote, and absurdly futile.
A magician's assistant
sparked with a thin powder
enchanting one who
stripped part of the book.

Compressed fathom of liquor
like a weariness after exertion.
Lavish caresses upon.
Graze, twist,
roll wool on the circular rim of
the thighbone.
Across the river, ardent
ferry man. Go and
bring back
between the filament,
small root
Of feverfew.
Threadlike, feeling silk
sew up
malleable fingers of
spirit of hydrogen
and glow.

Bellow, like a small wind
of flakes.
Maker of arrows
make a bend, flicker of passage
of fragments of floating ice
inundate the room, Goddess of Flowers,
Flora
glide along a stream
of handwriting.
    Copious, rhetorical duct of
fluent paper
    or end of the book
in two folios
    little bags
of refraction, I
bathe, take time by the forelock
fabricate to eternity
pen with a reservoir of ink.

Quantify that is not an integer
I hire a cargo ship
go habitually to
his doctrine. A small fly
in a spiral lock of hair
at the beginning of the book
hope, unfurnished room, fructifying
fat apparatus fusible
at both ends, the knot on nerve.
Passage of the flesh
an intoxicant, inflamed woman's
blouse.
Room on the top floor
catch breath with open mouth
down the gauntlet of wine
translucent small person,
Japanese dancing girl
of the zodiac
30 years of formation
wary of books, plaything,

Indian butter, ghost, convex thing
thinly with gold

encircle a wandering
girl, measures across
the bride and
glacier. Bright twilight, poet,
white of an egg, shine faintly
sphere
    gathered, make glorious,
the tongue, which emits green light.

Fed to the full, go down, descend
read, become ruined,
go to the wall, goatling.
Going, a gondolier
Good-bye, worker, goldilocks.
In the morning
grind love
between hell and thigh
    feel about
the luxuriant grotto
lie prostrate
    stop the seawater
pivot
conjecture
gyrate.

Practice hagiolatry.

Falling from cloud a
split halo black
the tree she inhabited, her
style of writing
transient, in a cart
joined by sweat stains
worked by hand.
The mistake of writing
twice harmonic
harlequin, haul this instrument
of hemp leaves
of a fastening
to the shaft
mount & dried
discourse. Listen to that
habitude. 100 liters of
doctrine.

In the next world or the map of it
rupture
the high steel
Heporous,
point of abutment, the seed,
hinge, medicinal hour.
I am busy swimming.

I am digging up weeds
with scarlet berries.
Excavate
homeopathy collected by bees
a little man
of the same kind
maker of spoons,
      receive
a nymph in 60 minutes
husband your hurdy gurdy
Pindar,
as last is put first.

SECRET INK

"Transposing a fact of nature
  in its quivering near disappearance"
                    MALLARMÉ

A fact is whatever
it folds, parenthetically.
a table to a grasshopper.
Imbedded, a trilobite.
Thoughts nuzzle
or swim off alone
to peer over an edge.
What incident coagulated these ideas?
What silt slowly hardened
formed in pockets under great pressure

perhaps you are growing a crystal
made from alum and glass
warm water and a thread

evaporation is the key
an element
you once found necessary the derision
of the fact
made by your own mouth
tuned to its own destruction.

No, duration is the key
29 and ½ days
there is no blue light to reflect
use a blindfold and follow
first cut the wood
then crawl up a weed
of *progression and unfolding.*

The actual circumference is 24, 901 miles
the light shifts and flickers
as you walk through the sky and get lost
towards a *poetry of destruction*
her tears dim her luster
The essential work
looks like it won't work
across both diagonals depression
of a waxing, growing crescent
having flared burnt itself out
and the earth is seen slowly
blotting the book.

Manifold, self-multiplying
you are facing north
this precious stone set in the silver sea
could not be lit
though there was charring
the tentacles of the written
like elaborated yellow green light.
A tiny bleeding hole
it opens the way to what is
and never could be.

The hand releases the third ball
the light from Proxima Centauri
the weight of the poem
the one vibratory, the other elocutive
the answer is:
gravity.
The game ends when the ground is filled.
Urine will work as a secret ink.
Avoid setting fire to the paper as you write:
the army will land at midnight.
Authorless, we used milk
to attach to the battery
each layer should be insulated
when it does not reflect someone
who might have made it
dangling into dark space
human accessories
uneasy lies the hand
on a narrow slope.
Sliding transfusions on an hourglass shaped closure
which is always past or future
a binding condensation.

A gyroscope is invaluable
the universal means of finding position
in insoluble contradiction behind its
visible presence.
North by northwest
this shadow can be a guide.
A passage, an interval
and as many methods as you can.

Chance cannot be overcome.
Yet one pair, change three cards
Odds to improve to two pairs.
The chances of a good hand.
are increased by wild cards.
The presence of its infinitely problematic future
existing before it can exist.
Is this the same, then, the cohabiting
that by precious possibility
becomes actual.

I move my tongue on dry lip.
In the late afternoon sun
see a bottle filled with strips of paper
written on with words.
I don't know if chance
is the paper, the bottle
or the hand that dips
into an array
of elements,
particles and a black leather book.
Work backwards until an impulse
becomes chance. Cohabitation
an interval of empty
before it becomes actual
just as this morning's length
is prolonged in yellow streaks, wobbly
in the trembling dimension of its path.
Facing the mirror
that is the multiplying book
circumference shifts
cross diagonals of progression.
There is no blue light to reflect
only an embankment in the center
a slope rimmed by resulting force
everything shivering as the crystal is.

BLAISEDELL CELLOPHANE

All over the spoon the red ink flowed.
A syrup for an extremity of consciousness
I wrote, then eradicated it, then absolved it.
The snow, falling outside, is a chain
of molecules that seem continuous.
Every folded piece of white paper
cut with stubby scissors
is a negative lace
seen through the cut hole. The whole world a splinter
which is what it seems
to the ice queen
until she felled the splinter.
Or it grew and enveloped
the instruction to
first remove the cinder in thy own.

How fatigued they must become
in fairy tales,
to live out the terrible fate of commandments
or else twist them or else remake them
to the oldest purposes. No wonder
I've grown a hump and made friends with the trolls.
For it has snowed all night
and the curtains are long red streaks
drawn with a crayon on the wall
and if you walk on the white
trapezoidal bridge
between vacancies
you may look down in to the gorge
of everything and all the fairly tales
happen simultaneously
in the multiplex of the crystal
in which red crimson was
a warning and a realization of the evidence
of a heart's life and its terrible finale.
Blood grew like hair in that world
emitted from a mouth that spoke from a tree
sprayed across a page of flesh
a tracery, a ribbon, a remorseful string

of DNA of fire the color
in the room
that binds the snow
in a single drawn
gush of a line the story
tried to follow until something else
took over, tracks on the ice.

And it was then I read in the old cracked dictionary
Of the alge-marines, the guignol,
The gargouele and fosile, le chapiteau d´un cirque,
The salamandre, le pariessiene, un
métropole and menthe.
I listened for the scraping of the plow
which would erase what was drawn on the page.
This was not the end, however.
I drag a red crayon
over the witch's crimson mouth.
As everybody knows, afterwards
comes the eyes and then the eyebrows
and then the nose and then the neck and then the
        sun and then the moon.
    The radio is on.

Outside a deep wavery curtain
blows restlessly down the avenue.
I have to set out
With fur lined mukluks and a sled
and a miniature telephone to
the eclole bilingue in
"Arlington Massachusetts."
I had passed there one night before
and from a ground floor window
a woman was sitting inside a room behind
        transparent curtains
and called "take a look at these books
which are worth more than any tv." and
I had vowed one day to return
never dreaming it would be in the middle of
        the night in winter
When I would finally go to school.

GLASS OF AN HOUR

For Lynn Behrendt

Pertaining to uncles
this matter is of early, local Bishops.
    That is, unpolished ashy,
spoken secretly
as the word *avuncular* seems to suggest
jokes at breakfast half forgotten.
Yet, the Bishop returns
as refraction
the ploughed land
passed in a car in Georgia
the honeycomb of a dream
in which everything lost returns in a new form
of verdigris of old buildings in Brooklyn
washed in rain that green is, the inside of a calyx.
Followed the Dog Star all winter
our eyelids thick figs, fleshy cup
of the honeysuckle plant. In twilight
super abnormal perceptions act up.
Dove colored afternoon, I have been at the crossroads

crying for the Dauphin of France
having turned away
from useful knowledge or its citizens.
Palindrome, to see the whetstone finally
the whitish color of the deacon's leg
has a leathery appearance.
Puncture the skin
and find twelve-stone fruits,
the sublime embossing of desire.
Such atmosphere conditions my
elegies, banquets and charity.

Ivory colored as a jellyfish, these letters
pertain to lightning.
Spongy galactic,
the West Wind comes.
Undressing is like carving
due to the earth's rotation.
The cable of my arms
attached to forceps
opens the window. Tricky yesterday,
the period between sleep and wakefulness.
The glass of an hour.
The drowsy lobsters of alchemy

Inscribed on thin plates
the larval matrix your aunt
is divinely inspired also in the morning.
The Mallow Family
of spiritualist's
commands the mistletoe
welding slugs
to get to the broth. Rhyming
three syllables
with the morsel
of the mucus
that is the cutting edge
of the knife, the spinal cord
of the nacreous
the knitting of moss-like
flaxen memory.

My birthday came and went
a vast period of embryonic siege.
I derived oil
in the high temperature hospital.
With thread, suffused my
number nine stepmother
the master teacher along the female line

who commands the hand to
the back of the neck
makes bread from poppies, existence
from names, anatomical walls,
edible songbirds, the scrotum,
asteroids,
the ordeal.
Near the midriff the underground water
the speech
the longitudinal nightingale
the comb like sounds
issued in flying nets, the inveterate
corner of the mouth.
People walk
the measure of time
the joint effect of sun and saliva.

In dark rooms persist
as scriptoria serum.
The sisters
pertaining to caves
the surface of the earth
sweat glands
the extravagance of antimony.

Sometimes, I can't make much direction
at the conjunction
of surnames, the cobbling of amber
to figures
antidotes to a thesis
derived from yew trees
a quicksand of random events
like pillars in crepuscular time and space
the pulse of atoms
cubic capacity of the voice.
My dirge belongs to a proverb
results from singing a chain of eclogues
in the dice game of the whirlpool.

THE LAST FLOWER ON EARTH

You have to ask: What do I want from this poem?
You have to let the poem jerk your head around.
You have to tell the poem to take you away from here
But stay with the poem in this uncomfortable singular place
Where the flies and moths co-exist.
Take the smallest white wax worm from the plastic cup
And pray for it is fed to a leopard gecko who snaps
With her perfect little jaw at the worm and devours it.
Notice two sturdy brown leather suitcases from the 1940.
Notice bevelled blue glass on a knotted black string and
That the wind abrubtly shifts to cool.
In the final conclusion, at the end of the rope, in the most
Extreme circumstance of trying, trying to remember
The shape of something, expectations finally break down.
I try to give the poem flowers because I want the poem
To give me flowers. The poem sends a woman to open
The glass door. She is carrying a yellow, artificial daffodil
As though it is the representation of the last flower
On earth. She is thin and wears a sleeveless tank top
And her brown skin is shiny. I say: Karen, I won't be here

Tomorrow, please come and see me the next day.
She turns her head and looks at me and her eye
Is a huge brown pond through her bifocal eyeglasses.
I'm not coming to see you, she says and walks past.
I want the poem to let me have a new baby, I guess.
Why else would me and another, unseen woman,
In a poem help a third woman to birth a baby
On cement stairs. We are arguing if the swelling in her stomach
Breaking through is a baby. I am ecstatic when I see its head,
The size of a wet puppy head or a glass lightbulb.
I want nature to be seen in my poem as a slice,
A shard, an element obliquely
Encompassing logic.
Instead, the poem sends a map
Of the United States in the NY Times.
Each state is colored a bright coral.
The United States looks enraged,
Like a lobster taking out of a pan of boiling water..
The poem says:
You can't have any lobster, you stupid, hungry poet.
No lobster with chutney and Mersault like in Wallace Steven's
Poem. The poem eradicates food.
Says go trudge with these people

Who are walking for many many miles over the dirt
and sand.
To find something to eat and drink at a U.N. station.
The poem steals my cell phone
And says listen very carefully to the sounds of these
thundering trucks
And stop talking.
I ask the poem, finally, what can
I learn and the poem
Takes all the trucks away and the avenue
Sounds like a vibrating river.
The poem is making the world smell
Wet and cool at four in the morning.
I go and look for my lover in the poem
But when I open the door
Everything is completely dark and hot and silent.
A man is yelling in Kryole now. Is this my lover?
He goes away, the voice , an instrument
Speaking unintelligibly pauses. The poem tells
Me to to stop looking and go away too.
I want to have the moon in my poem.
I try and see the moon out of the window through
the branches.

Last night the moon was a creamy antique disk
And now is absent.
Like food, it is obliterated. In a fit of nostalgia,
I try to destroy people, food, the room, flowers
And landscapes.
Everything is blackness, a baby has been
Born and the poem is utterly original,
I tell myself. An abstraction
Of meshed textures and
Asymmetrical utterances the
Shape of an air conditioner emission.
What does that look like?
A grayish dirty cloud of micro particles.
That spreads and bathes us in warm air.
As we stand on the other side of the air conditioner
Where vents and coils are blowing air on our faces.
Then the poem sends a white monster to lick the street clean
And it eats up my original poem.
However, the poem sends the moon, finally,
As a tiny picture, previously unnoticed, on a bookshelf.
There it is: a feminized, worried looking male
Face imprinted on a bluish crescent in a blue sky, La Luna
Next to a black boot, La Bota, in a yellow sky.
La Luna hangs over la Corizon, a hunk of red meat

And over El Musico, the poet in his yellow pants and who carrys
His yellow guitar. El Musico
Stands in a doorway, probably waiting for a poem, the big dummy.
The poem says you go on standing there. Here's someone
To keep you company: El Soldado, who stands with his big gun
And wears his green pants. Each in their own square
Looking blankly out of the frame.
They will never know that over their head hangs
La Sandia, the watermelon, which kind of looks like El Corizon,
Which is also red, meaty,and imbedded with black seeds.

Bentley, Scott. *The Occasional Tables.*

Bouchard, Daniel. *Diminutive Revolutions.*

Bouchard, Daniel. *Some Mountains Removed.*

Brennan, Sherry. *Of Poems and Their Antecedents.*

Carey, Steve. *Selected Poems.*

Cariaga, Catalina. *Cultural Evidence.*

Carll, Steve, and Bill Marsh. *Tao Drops I Change.*

Davis, Jordan, and Sarah Manguso. (Eds.)
    Free Radicals: American Poets Before Their First Books.

Dinh, Linh. *All Around What Empties Out.*

Edwards, Kari. *A Day in the Life of P.*

Elliot, Joe. *Opposable Thumbs.*

Evans, Brett. *After School Sessions.*

Fitterman, Robert, and Dirk Rowntree. *War, the Musical.*

Friedlander, Benjamin. *The Missing Occasion of Saying Yes.*

Guthrie, Camille. *In Captivity.*

Guthrie, Camille. *The Master Thief.*

Harrison, Roberto. *Os.*

Hofer, Jen. *Slide Rule.*

Holloway, Rob. *Permit.*